# Getting Fired Up!
A Manual for Self Exploration in Your Time of Job or Life Change

## Sean Ashleigh Russell

MODERNISTA PRESS
LONDON   BARCELONA   NEW YORK   MIAMI   DALLAS

Copyright © 2012 by Sean Ashleigh Russell

Getting Fired Up! A Manual for Self-Exploration in Your Time of Job Change or life Transition/Sean Ashleigh Russell.-1$^{st}$ ed., Paperback – Published 2012, ISBN: 978-1-300-38837-1

All rights reserved.

10 9 8 7 6 5 4 3 2 1

Printed in the United States of America

For my daughter Ariella-Valentina, inspiration, angel, and lover of books.

And, my husband, Alec, who is my "equilibrium" and I am happy to be your "dolce" after all these years.

Also, to the Chinese Year of the Dragon and igniting the fire within.

**Table of Contents:**

| | | |
|---|---|---|
| Author Note | | 8 |
| I. | Foreword | 9 |
| II. | About the Author | 11 |
| III. | Introduction | 20 |
| IV. | Honest Self-Evaluation | 26 |
| V. | The Best Revenge is Success | 30 |
| VI. | Personality Type vs. Potential Career Paths | 34 |
| VII. | 10 Signs You Are Getting Fired | 41 |
| VIII. | Navigation Techniques To Gain Control | 46 |
| IX. | Getting Fired, the Upside? | 51 |
| X. | Who Cares What Others Think! | 58 |
| XI. | Next Steps, Resources & Knowing Ask for Help | 61 |
| XII. | Know Thy Self | 69 |
| XIII. | Ego & You Are Not Your Job | 83 |
| XIV. | Case Studies | 91 |
| XV. | Planning Worksheets | 118 |
| XVI. | Daily Practice of Control & Self-discipline | 128 |

| XVII. | Keep Clarity in Your Priorities & Launch a Personal Public Relations Campaign | 131 |
| XVIII. | The Plan: 1 Month, 6 Months, 1 Year, 3 Years | 136 |
| XIX. | Unexpected Detours | 150 |
| XX. | Re-evaluate | 152 |
| XXI. | Stay Fired Up! | 171 |
| XXII. | Credits | 181 |
| XXIII. | Notes | 184 |

## Author Note

Make **Getting Fired Up!** the *"Go To" Book*. **Keep it on hand to read** when you are waiting for the train or have a moment before a job interview or meeting. It's a *MANUAL* so it's *meant to be dog-eared, highlighted and scribbled in.*

It is light weight, portable and the dragon imagery is added inspiration. On my desk at my home office, I have a small plastic Hello Kitty figurine and a rubber dragon. They represent the dualities in my life of motherhood and professional life, but they both motivate me in different ways. Use whatever is meaningful to you to reinforce a positive disposition as this has a way of overshadowing negative thoughts.

**Use it for lists and planning.** When negative thoughts creep in, remind yourself that you are **Getting Fired Up!** for *positive change and transition in your life.*

I.    Foreword

I wrote this exploratory guide from the heart, but it is meant for anyone struggling with a firing, lay-off, life change or other emotional strain. Provided are the tools to begin to work from the brain, rather than the emotional heart.

Like a relationship break-up, a divorce or other type of separation, losing a job can be a difficult situation to cope with. The earlier you can begin to differentiate between the logical pieces of what happened versus the emotional side, the faster you can move forward in your life.

This book was intended to serve as a guide with thought provoking questions to answer honestly so that you can live your authentic life, not a life that is plotted for appearances sake nor a life served to attain a large job title, ego driven motivation or a false sense of worth.

My grandfather taught me to always have a "nice occasion" outfit on hand as you never know what occasion may arise and it would be a shame to miss an opportunity because of the lack of appropriate attire. The look of disappointment before church on a summer Sunday in Palm Beach Gardens was too much to bear when he asked: "Are you going to wear *that*?" Since then, I have always packed with thoughtful intent. While our outer wear IS important in our modern world, it is our inner selves that really matter and we need to constantly take inventory.

In K.C. Cole's book **First You Build a Cloud**, she writes: "Perception, after all, is a very *active* process. We do not just sit around waiting for information to rain down on us. We go out and get it. In the process, we alter it and even create it." I suggest you dress for success, **mentally**. Being prepared with rain gear through the storms of a lay off can get you FIRED UP and onto a sunny path much faster.

II.     About the Author

I started working as early as I could. At the age of eight, I started an underground newspaper in the apartment complex I lived with my single mother in San Antonio, Texas. I teamed up with an eighteen-year-old boy who lived nearby. Obviously, when I brought him home to work on the paper, my mother was shocked, but we were both determined journalists. We took the paper as far as we could without having investors to take the publication to the next level. That was the start of my passion for journalism.

Like most kids, I went through a long list of professions that I was aspiring to pursue as I got older. It included pilot, lawyer, veterinarian, journalist and actress. When it came to this decision in college, I chose Journalism as I enjoyed writing, but I was not clear of the capacity in which I would work until I later had an internship at a television station and then, later would decide I didn't fit in television.

After college, the reality of a competitive job market was compounded by a hard economy and I continued to wait tables at a restaurant bar making more money than I did in television, advertising or the many other jobs I held.

In my mid-twenties, I was working in marketing administration at a very large computer company. The company went through a large merger and was the acquired company. The entire marketing department was laid-off, including my boss the Director of Marketing, except me. I was offered a salary increase and my responsibility level was to be much higher (basically the job description of ten former employees). While I saw the opportunity in this, I also had another job offer from a large publishing company based in San Diego and I was to take a lead in the start-up Dallas/Houston Magazines.

The pay was low, but I had a passion for the industry and the role I took on. This was a huge learning experience for me and I enjoyed the work, but in the midst of this job, I was side tracked by the planning of my wedding. After the wedding, my husband and I had started a business in the pet product supply industry and it was ready to be taken to the next level. He was much occupied with his main business, a recording studio and I wanted to run with the start-up.

Again, I learned much about manufacturing in China, international distribution, logistics and electronics. Unfortunately, in the divorce, I learned more about business partnership agreements, financial statements and the like.

After the divorce, I immediately began another job, which was decent pay, but completely unrewarding. I had a brief stint at a financial institution where I worked as a temporary worker. I applied and successfully interviewed for the head of the communications department, locally. Although I was an internal hire, they were under the impression that I was a higher level employee at the company and when they learned that I was a temporary employee in a lower level position, I was told that I needed an MBA for this position.

I got another job, again, it wasn't a great match, but I had to pay the bills. I also decided to buy a house and get my realtors license and gain more control of my career. I completed my classes, passed the state exam and I was approved for my mortgage with my current job.

I closed on the deal with my realtor and we split the commission.

My employer learned I wanted to do real estate on the side and they let me go from the company just months after I had a new mortgage.

I took night classes in graduate school, leased apartments by day and kept purging ahead.

My personal life was stagnating, so I focused more on my professional life. I began working with Shiseido Cosmetics and Saks Fifth Avenue to launch a new line of skin care. Just as that began to take off, I decided that I wanted to move to the

Northeast and pursue more opportunities out there. At the same time, I met my now husband and we began a long distance dating relationship for six months until I sold my house and made the move 1,800 miles Northeast.

With the studio rental apartment in Boston being three times my former Dallas mortgage and winter fast approaching, I realized the dream of living abroad may be an ideal decision. I found an opportunity to start an American franchise in Catalonia and my then boyfriend was onboard as he had family there and had wanted to return to live.

After flights back to Texas (Waco) for training, I embarked on a journey to change countries, start a new business, learn two new languages, live in Europe with my boyfriend all in the pursuit of happiness and life balance.

Nobody I told was shocked. Nobody really even questioned what I was doing. In retrospect, that seems odd to me, but I am a determined independent adventure seeking little Sagittarius and I have a strong will.

Like I mention in later chapters, doing all of these things at once may not have been the best choice, but ultimately it has worked out for me and I am currently living a fulfilling life with no regrets.

The job losses, lay-offs and firings have opened doors for professional growth. The ending of relationships, downward economies and personal challenges facilitated life change that was uncomfortable, but ultimately proved to be rewarding.

Since living in Europe over a decade, I have worked in corporate jobs, started a family, ran a marathon, and started several successful businesses.

\*\*\*\*\*\*\*\*\*\*\*\*\*\*\*\*\*\*\*\*\*\*\*\*\*\*\*\*\*\*\*\*\*\*\*\*\*\*\*\*\*\*\*\*\*\*

Credentials:

Author of "For Flexibility, Own More Than One Business" Women Entrepreneur Magazine, 2009

Featured as a Woman of the World, Capitalist Chicks, 2008

Contributor to the book "Workaholic No More," author, Jennifer Blair, 2008

Featured Blogger: www.artofbusinessspeaking.com, 2007

Founder of Curves for Women franchise, Catalonia, Spain, 2002

Published Due Diligence Guidelines – distributed by grad school academia, 2000

Speaker for various women entrepreneur television, radio shows, blogs and print media.

**Sean Ashleigh Russell is an American expat who lives along the coast overlooking the Mediterranean in Barcelona Spain**, with her husband, Alec, and daughter, Ariella Valentina, where she divides her time between writing, communications consulting, travel, kite sailing, wine export and the constant quest for maintaining Dolce Equilibrium (the name of her former company), which means "sweet balance," in Italian.

Ashleigh was born in the Midwest, lived in the Southwest and Northeast regions of the United States as well as Australia and has lived in Spain for over a decade. **She has written a bilingual children's book.**

**Ashleigh joins the ranks** of other **impressive business writers with more than 20 years of experience in strategic planning, marketing and operations for private and public companies, and extensive experience in the media, social media, communications, and services industries.** Ashleigh has **worked in television**, as an intern/associate producer for a talk show at **NBC** in Dallas, Texas. She has also worked in

**publishing, sales, advertising, public relations and real estate.** Aside from her communications endeavors, she **co-founded a pet product supply company** (Wordy Birdy) and served as public relations chairperson on the Board of Directors for a non-profit organization (T.R.O.T) which helps the disabled through a program of equine therapy. She **started the first Curves For Women franchise** (Curvas) in Catalonia, Spain. She has a journalism degree from Texas Christian University and an MBA from the University of Dallas.

Presently, she is founder of **Enaj-et-Trois**, a natural skincare line and she continues in her roles as Marathon Mom and Serial Entrepreneur.

III.     Introduction

We all come from diverse circumstances and none are more valid than others, just different.  You probably have come across many people in life who appear to have it all.  In other words, they were born into a wealthy family or had a very high I.Q. or had an innate sense of discipline which enables them to secure a full scholarship or other advantage. Meanwhile, you work very hard to achieve what you can, but you are faced with student loans, not having connections for dream jobs, and facing an uphill battle along the way, which makes your drive for success waiver on a daily basis.

To add insult to injury, you see those same people with life advantages throw away many opportunities given to them as they voluntarily self-destruct with drugs, alcohol or other toxic addictions.

The thing to recognize here is that life is not fair. It is what it is. The faster you can recognize this and accept it, the better off you will be. It sounds simple, but it is within our nature to fight these universal laws. We want explanations, we crave equality and whether we will admit this or not, we want others to sympathize with our plight.

This is not double talk rhetoric which you will find in many self-help books on the market today. This is a process in which the aim is to gain clarity of your professional goals and how they fit into your life purpose and how to develop an action plan to get you closer to turning your dreams into a reality.

How does all of this relate to getting fired? Some of these things I have described are real circumstances or situational variances, most of which you have no real control over. If we did have control over these, I suspect that many of us would wish to be born into a royal family or to have been blessed with keen talents or other such circumstances. These things are not likely to change; however, I continue to play the lottery as I know statistically speaking, while not probable, there is a possibility to win.

So, this brings us to why it is important to recognize these factors with such clarity. I will suggest to you that you possess something that gives you the power to control these surroundings and events. I suggest to you that while you may not be able to control much you are presented within life, there is one very important facet you are able to control and I guarantee it has the power to change everything in your life.

This magical item I allude to is, simply, your perception. The ability to control this can have substantial impact on the chains of events in your life. For instance, you have been fired. You are upset and feel violated or you feel life is unfair and you worry how you will pay your bills. These thoughts seem appropriate to you and others may even support you with sympathy and agree with you that you have been wronged. Understandably, these members of your support system are well intentioned, but they are doing you a disservice.

Not only are they re-enforcing a myth, but they are slowing your process for change by telling you what you want to hear and not telling you what you need to hear. But, you worked very hard on a project that went wrong and your boss blamed everything on you when it was clear to you it was not your fault, then, you were fired.

This is your side of the story. Maybe your boss perceives the mistakes in the projects as belonging to you and he or she feels violated for investing in an employee who did not turn out to be the best choice. It could also be that your boss really does not think you did anything wrong, but he or she is under intense pressure to eliminate headcount and had already decided it had to be you and this project was an easy way to do this dirty work.

All of what you have read will come together now with clarity. One, it does not really matter if you were fired for right or wrong reasons. You are not a rock star or part of the royal family. This is how it is as life is not fair, accept it.

Two, you cannot control others perception. Of course, you can influence it, but ultimately, they have final control.

Three, you make choices which continue to have a spiralling effect on your life. If you choose to go into your boss' office after he or she has fired you and you choose to yell an explicative at him or her, you must live with the repercussions of that choice. For example, if you choose to play victim and tell everyone for months how unfair life is, then, you have chosen to postpone your potential for happiness and the progression to achieve your goals even more.

Four, what you can control is to choose how you will perceive the situation. That job was actually quite stressful and I have wanted to make a change for some time. The day-to-day energy I exerted to deal with an unreasonable boss left me feeling depleted at the end of the day and I felt powerless and unrewarded for the work I was doing.

Does this mean you should go into your former boss' office and thank this person for firing you? No. Does this mean if you were victim to sexual harassment or other such unacceptable circumstances, you should just rationalize the previous stated fact that life is unfair and not pursue a path for justice? No.

I will communicate in later chapters the difference between accepting the hand that is dealt to you and when to call the dealer out for cheating behaviour. This is an important distinction, but as your clarity increases, you will be able to discern the difference between making decisions which will empower you and decisions which will either be destructive or slow your progress.

IV.    Honest Self-Evaluation

The more you can understand your self and access internal traits honestly and without self judgement, the better equipped you become to recognize the best career path choice.

Understand, it *is* a choice to not actively make a choice. If you were not one of the very fortunate ones to be born with an outstanding talent, such as performing or superior athleticism, possibly you had a clear goal and you worked very hard to achieve it. For example, since you were a young child, you always loved animals and you just knew that when you got older and the time came to make a career choice, you would be a veterinarian.

As you grew older, your parents were supportive of your ambition and you also had a very clear vision of what actions you needed to take to make your professional dream become a reality. You studied hard and you participated in all of the necessary education and training to become a veterinarian. Fast forward five or ten years and you are a happily practicing veterinarian.

Now, what if it was not in the cards for you to be a rock star or a Heisman trophy winner and what if you never had a clear vision of what you would like to do with your life, professionally speaking?

Perhaps you graduated from university and assumed that was achievement enough. You reasoned that most students do not end up practicing the profession they study for in college, so why should you be any different?

Okay, fast forward a few years after college and you have been struggling to find a job and by this time, you have ruled out a career in retail, administration, sales and teaching.

You rationalize that you are now looking for something else because you were not lucky enough to get that perfect job or the market is very bad, and so on.

Although these things may be a reality, but the real reason you are without a professional path is that you CHOSE not to make a career choice. THAT was your decision. As passive as it was, it was the choice that you made and all of the following decisions and events stemmed from this choice not to decide clearly.

Now, I know you may say in your defense that your college room-mate chose to be a lawyer and invested much into that choice and now he is a bartender at the local pub in his home town.

And, of course, in your consequent efforts of not making a clear career choice, you gained knowledge in diverse facets of many professions and industries. Even if you had to work a lot of jobs to figure out what you did not want to do, it's a type of process of elimination and it gets you closer to your calling.

The purpose in illustrating your lack of proactive decision-making is not to bruise your already inflamed ego more, but to show you how to get from Point A to Point B faster and more efficiently in your next professional transition period. Because we learn from our mistakes, we build character when faced with difficult life challenges and we grow as human beings when confronted with obstacles, the key is to learn what we can and keep moving forward, while minimizing bouts of depression or dangerous detours of revenge.

## V. The Best Revenge is Success

Success is something that is achieved, but it is not constant. If you take a closer look at people who have been successful, you will see that they have experienced some or a lot of failure prior to achieving a successful status. As with life, this status is ever-changing.

You can be on top one moment and at the bottom the next. With understanding this, comes power as you have the power to regulate the amount of energies to devote to what you perceive as an unsuccessful period of time.

If you know one thing almost always has to happen before the other, then why not cherish your failures as well? I am not suggesting you celebrate a demotion at work or a challenge in starting your own business, but by changing the way you perceive events along the way, you can improve the journey and often reach your goals faster.

It is within the failures and the challenges that we have the most growth and learning, so to not place value on these experiences is a mistake.

The other facet to this learning is that with age and life experiences comes clarity. Something perceived as a failure at twenty years old may turn out to have been the leading cause to much happiness and success much later in life.

For example, you are fired from a job you loved, but it propels you into taking on higher education which later leads you into a career that is much more satisfying and rewarding than the job you were fired from.

Sometimes life dictates changes in our careers that were unpredictable despite the fact that we believe we have devised a foolproof plan to attain success.

I interviewed a woman who started a family much faster than she had realized any career success. She resented the challenging moments and felt she was missing out on her professional track. She went on to start what is now a highly successful gourmet food company. She decided to channel the energy into things that she COULD do and to stop focusing on what she thought she could not do and it proved to be the defining action in her success.

The success is what is authentic to you not what others perceive success to be for you. In this I mean that if you get fired from a job only to get a higher pay job with a competitor and you want to make sure that your former company is aware of this, you need to recognize that this is an ego-driven thought. If your high school reunion is approaching and you want to make sure that anyone who had wronged you in high school saw how fabulous you had become, you are wasting your energies.

One does not need to broadcast true success. It comes from within. It comes from being a good mother or father or working hard to achieve good things in life. When you feel authentically successful or happy in life, you want to share that with others but from a place of good intent and not ego.

If you are driven from a place of ego, then it is best to re-evaluate what is important in your life and how you can best achieve those things in the most honest fashion. If the outward success does not align with what others perceive is success, but you honor your authentic inner path, than you are successful.

## VI. Personality Type(s) Vs. Potential Career Paths

I am going to outline distinct personality types and demonstrate the importance of recognizing your type and how it relates to the job selection process. When navigated more effectively on the forefront, the odds that you will have to deal with involuntary dismissal significantly curves to your favour.

Please note that if you fit into more than one arch type or personality, this does not mean that you have multiple personalities. It only signifies that you overlap traits or characteristics from more than one and this should play into your decision making process.

Also, look at these arch types as a guide only. I am not a scientist and this type of self exploration requires constant thought and attention to "self" as suggested. One other useful tip before we begin, look at this process without judgement. For instance, when a person is unable to cope well with routine everyday, it does not signify a person with stability problems. It only shows that a person who likes routine, for example, in an office environment, may be better equipped to handle or excel in a career in this environment than a person who would feel like a caged animal going to an office and working the same hours day after day. However, the caged animal may make an exceptional entrepreneur and achieve much success in building a business working sporadic hours with unpredictable surroundings.

Archetypes:

I. Not a team player
II. Consistent worker
III. Gets bored, needs challenge
IV. Diplomat

These are not meant to be complex theories, but simple names offering insight to the human psyche. They are relatable terms to identify your personality type and how it corresponds to potential job satisfaction, which is directly correlated to success. The clearer this can become, the potential for experiencing getting fired can be decreased. The hope is that your professional choices can be expedited to reach your goals faster.

Let's begin with Archetype I. You are the opposite of a team player. Do not let the judgement creep in as many people automatically have the predisposition to assume that this is a negative trait. And, often, this allows stigmas to creep in and then you are not able to do a fair self-assessment, which prevents you from doing the work to facilitate your best outcome.

Just because you can admit you do not like working with other people, this does not make you a bad hire or someone who should work on this characteristic. Of course, we all must work with people at different stages in our professional paths, but there are certainly different capacities in which to do this. For example, if this describes you, it may not be the best choice for you to work as a project manager in a large corporate climate. You may feel frustrated having to work with cross-teams and be a part of the decision-making process in a team environment.

However, you may be the ideal candidate to be a real estate agent where you primarily rely on yourself to do the marketing and sales. Of course, you have to deal with people, you cannot avoid this entirely, but it would be a less restrictive team environment and may offer interaction with one or two people at one time versus ongoing groups.

Archetype II is the consistent worker. This sounds boring and one might presume this person is a follower, not a leader. However, I have had many friends who fit this type who have had great success in their chosen professional paths because of this trait.

For instance, one of my friends started a job at a large telecom company just after completing university. She began in an entry-level role and while she had slow progression, it was sure and steady. Now, after twenty years at that company, she has one of the highest level executive positions in the company. While her contemporaries (me included) experienced many job and even full blown career changes in those same twenty years, she endured what seemed to be slow promotions and monotonous work. But, she thrived on the stability and cherished her role. Also, within those twenty years, her employee invested stock program, slowly, then quickly experienced huge gains, which also resulted in a huge pay-off for her many years of slowly vesting a small, consistent amount into the program.

Archetype III gets bored and needs challenge. This person could be judged as a flake or someone who is spontaneous and challenges authority. But, we are not judging, right? On the flip side, this personality type encompasses many well-known inventors and entrepreneurs who have impacted our popular culture with the likes of apples, blueberries and other well-known fruity inventions.

This person would probably not do well within a structure of yearly evaluations, such as teaching or the monotony of working in a manufacturing plant.

This person could own and manage a business where things are changing daily or another good choice may be working as a reporter for a magazine or newspaper in which the projects change daily.

Archetype IV is the diplomat. This person is well inclined to handle office politics and difficult people without breaking a sweat. While politics is an obvious choice for this personality type, this person can also do well in sales, government or social positions requiring finesse and control. If you know you get irritated or frustrated in situations easily, you should avoid a role which requires this natural bend.

Unacceptable Professional Situations versus Difficult Situations

Most of us will experience difficult work situations at one point or more likely, many points along our careers. These should be expected and navigated to your best ability. This means that making the right choices by restraining your emotional reactions, for example, may save you from a firing. If you have already gotten fired, you can navigate your best path by using your powers of perception and the strength of control you are learning about in this book.

However, there are the cases in which a person is faced with sexual harassment or verbal abuse or even worse. These, I do not suggest, you should accept, deal with and move on with quickly. These special circumstances require serious attention, support and when necessary, professional services.

VII.    10 Signs That You Are Getting Fired:

1) Suddenly, you are no longer in the loop. You are finding more and more that you are the last to know about normal operations or things specifically within your department.

2) You are given impossible projects by upper management for you to complete under difficult time constraints. These projects are there either to set you up for failure, thus, making a firing easier or to give you busy work until your replacement has either been trained or they have figured out what to do with your situation.

3) When you inquire about your role or projects, you are not given a response or it is a carefully verbalized response.

4) You just made a very big mistake and your gut instinct tells you that this is the perfect excuse for your boss to show you the door.

5) The attitude of your boss or co-workers changes. Suddenly, people are reacting differently to you, distant or possibly avoiding you all together.

6) You have had a bad formal review or you begin getting many reprimands in the form of written memos or frequent meetings.

7) You are hearing rumors.

8) Your company has recently down-sized, is about to go through a merger or experiencing tough economic times.

9) If you have been given a recent pay-cut or you are asked to compile a report showing your value.

10) Do not under any circumstances go into a meeting at your company which has the agenda to assure employees that they will not lose their jobs in an upcoming merger-acquisition, etc. It's simply a tactic to minimize fears and you should not buy into it. You also are probably not in the position to fight it with much success, but you can control your actions for an urgent pro-active job search!

It is hard to see the signs especially when you are not expecting it. Lay-offs can come as a surprise, but often there are rumors of the potential event and sometimes employees are informed the week or day of a lay-off.

In doing research for this book, I interviewed a man who had been at a company over twenty years and he was informed indirectly that Friday, Valentines Day would be the last day of work for himself, along with about fifty other employees.

He was at a point in his life that he could effectively retire, but he knew he would want to continue to work in some capacity after this job ended.

Some of the employees new that this lay-off would happen, others did not and most did not know when it would occur. On Friday, this man brought in 100 cupcakes decorated with hearts and his personal email address attached to each wrapper. Not only was this a brilliant approach to this time of transition, but it immediately got him networking with his contemporaries and he later started a consultancy with one of the ladies from another department who had received his cupcake. By taking a proactive approach it reversed feelings of emotional helplessness and replaced those feelings with a sense of control.

So, my suggestion is to bring cupcakes when it is appropriate. Be creative in your approach to departure, but keep it positive.

VIII.     Navigation Techniques to Gain Control

You have been fired and you are still in the workplace. First and foremost, stay composed. If you feel like you are going to lose it, take yourself to the bathroom stall and get it out. If you have been given until the end of the day to clear your things, or even worse, the next hour, you must focus on the tasks ahead and do not allow your emotions to control your actions.

Most likely, you will have some paperwork and you will need to clear out personal belongings from your desk or cubicle. If it is a larger company, you may be asked to go to human resources and conduct an exit interview. You have control here. If you feel like you will either break down and cry or you are so stunned that you cannot express yourself effectively, you can tell your human resources contact that you would like to do an exit interview, but you would like to call to schedule it in the next few days as you feel it would be more productive for everyone. If they object, you do not have to do it and you can tell them that you have been fired and you choose not to do this interview.

Don't let others dictate to you the terms as everything is negotiable. Maybe they will hold your final pay-check until you do this interview, but in the larger picture, what is one or two days? The benefit in putting this off is to allow you to collect your thoughts and present your side of the situation. Knowing that even if you make a good case about how your performance has been superior, your fate has been cast and it will not change the situation. But, what it might do for you is to feel like you have had a voice and you will not play the victim in this challenge.

Do not under any circumstance, use explicative words to anyone in the office after you have been fired. This will only make you look bad. If you want to discuss this with a co-worker, get their personal phone number or email and do it there, but be aware that they are still working for the company and the perceived alliance may have loyalties elsewhere.

Also, do not let yourself do any physical damage to company property or any theft as this will most likely result in making a bad situation much worse. And, remember, we want to go the other way. We want to expedite things and get back on the path to happiness.

In this day and age, intellectual property is the most valuable resource a company has aside from human assets. In most cases, this property clearly remains under the ownership of the company. However, in some cases, such as sales jobs, the salesperson develops relationships with clients and that relationship is removed once that sales person is no longer in place. The rolodex of clients legally belongs to the employer, not the employee.

Do not be tempted to steal these clients from the company if you think you have been wrongly terminated. If you have a contract which indicates the non-compete duration, honour it. You do not want to deal with legal ramifications down the line.

You want to obtain the most control possible given the situation. Other co-workers may be experiencing transition as well, but you may not learn about it until later. The importance of understanding this possibility should prevent you from burning any bridges within the company.

As long as you maintain your reputation, you may be able to network at a later date and have more opportunities. You never know who will make a move to a larger company and be in a position to hire you or give you an inside reference. Your former co-worker may open his or her own business and think of you as a potential hire or partner. By limiting any exit damage, you keep your future options open.

I have found that by constructing a timeline of events, actions and outcomes, it helps to see more clearly how negative events lead to positive outcomes. The following is just an example of my own experiences that I mapped.

Utilize this re-framing technique to challenge internal dialogue and perception of the events in your life.

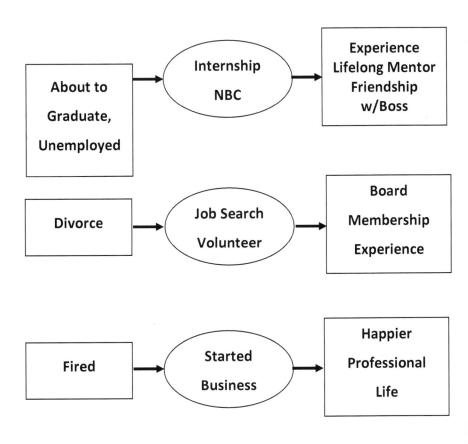

IX.   Getting Fired, the Upside?

You may not be ready for this chapter yet, so reference it when you are ready. Odds are that if you got fired, you probably were not that happy with your job to begin with, however, there are those rare circumstances when a person is completely blindsided by this chain of events and genuinely liked what he or she was doing professionally. I might suggest that this person look deeper in accessing honestly if he or she was good at the former role. Sometimes when we are still learning new things, we may have interest and be motivated to excel, but it is quite possible that our skills are not up to par. This is hard to admit to ourselves, but please understand that it does not equate to failure or inadequacy in any way. It is progress to recognize not only our strengths, but our weaknesses as well.

For the majority, a brief reflection on the former job, can lead to an overwhelming sensation of complete job dissatisfaction. There possibly were stretches of days, weeks or even years when you forced yourself to go to work. There was no question that if you won the lottery, you would quit your job.

While the investment of time varies with each stage in our lives, many of us spend the vast majority of our time working. This is followed by sleep and *then* time with family and friends. While many of us would like to think that family and friends are our priorities, it is not evident by our actions.

Again, this is a moment of truth. If you are asked by someone "What are your priorities in life?" And your answer is: "Spending time with my family, my health and hobbies like playing the guitar and sailing." And now for the truth part: You do enjoy spending time with your family, but due to work commitments and travel, it has been limited to time on the weekends, you once liked to play the guitar, but you have not really picked it up in over five years, you have only been sailing one time in your life and that was ten years ago.

Even worse, you watch about ten hours of television on the weekends, you tend to eat fast food and as far as your health is concerned, you have not been to the doctor in years. Could you possibly answer the person like the following? "What are your priorities in life?" "I like to consume unhealthy, processed food and watch television for the majority of my time, I work family in as I can after my job commitments and I am not active in any interests."

Of course you would not answer the question like this! When someone asks the question: "How are you?" You may say "fine, thank you," but you probably would not go into detail about all of your worries and problems, well, most of us would not do so!

The point I am trying to make is that you would probably feel much better about yourself being able to answer the way you would like your behaviour to be and know that your behaviour truly matches your words.

This is true in your job as well. We all would like to enjoy what we are spending most of our time on everyday. Sometimes it takes a brutal act like getting fired to make us realize that we are being less than honest with ourselves and it is time to step out of our comfort zone.

But, wait you are thinking that you WANT to like your job or career track, but at the moment you are in transition or in an entry-level position, school or clueless as to what you would be happy doing professionally, correct?

Let me remind you that it is a *process* and it will be in constant motion. This is where the other factor which was discussed earlier comes into play. That is your perception. You have control over that and if you perceive that the tough microbiology classes you are struggling with now will lead you to a happy career as a scientist, than you can be happy that you are on the path that is right for you.

Another example, if you are working for very little pay at Wal-Mart, but the hours you are scheduled allow you to work a non-paid internship as a sound engineer in a recording studio, then, you can feel good about that Wal-Mart clerk job as it is bringing you closer to your dream job.

If, however, you are working a job everyday that you do not enjoy and you are not working towards an exit strategy and plan to start something new, or even worse, you have not even explored any options, then you cannot honestly feel good about your choice.

And, please recall: Making no choice is in itself a choice. It is a bad one.

Let me remind you that very few lessons are learned purely from success. Most successful persons have learned much more from their failures.

I suggest to you that transition represents an opportunity for growth. Transition occurs at every life stage and in every realm of daily modern living. When you are younger, transition is part of natural growth. From babyhood to toddlerhood to teenage years, the mental, emotional and physical growth is obvious.

As we get older, transition often is a result of a choice we make. For instance, we plan for years to go off to university or we spend months planning our dream wedding. These transitions are life changing and full of growth opportunities.

So often we correlate transition with failure, especially with regards to professional life. For example: "Did you hear about Bob? He got laid off and now made a transition to consulting." But, Bob has a chance to experience things from a different perspective. Ten years later, he has grown his consultancy to a grand level and his previous co-worker has moved from a cubical to an office and had only a slight increase in salary.

Some people are bigger risk takers than others. I do not, however, believe that life is about playing it safe, avoiding change or limiting transitions. Obviously, the more calculated risks you take, the higher your chance of success will be.

While going to college and getting married result in positive phases of life transition, other transitions such as flunking out of school, divorce, job loss or death are certainly hard experiences, the silver lining is that this forced transition can lead to much greater things.

X.   Who Cares What Others Think!

If you are more evolved, you do not care what others think. However, as much as we fight it, we do seem to care about the opinions of others. The closer we can bring ourselves to not caring, the faster we will be able to bypass this wasted energy and achieve our goals. Until then, let us spend minimal time on this topic and develop a strategy to use until we are confident enough to do otherwise.

First of all, nobody knows the reality of your job, your marriage, or your fears more so than yourself. The girlfriend you vent to may understand some of your marital issues, but she does not get the complete picture as she has no idea what goes on behind closed doors or more to the point, in the minds of yourself and your husband. Your co-workers and boss might have an idea of how you view your job, but they may be entirely off base. Your shrink, your pastor, your friends may understand some of your fears, but all of us have deep emotions within us and very often we are not even in complete touch with them ourselves!

With this said, let's develop a pre-determined set of responses for your nagging mother-in-law, your friends at the country club, your old high school buddies and the new acquaintances you have yet to meet. I suggest that when you are faced with the question of "What do you do for a living?" and you have just been fired, laid off or quit your job by your own accord, you can simply answer "I am exploring new opportunities, " "I am taking a much needed break…vacation, etc.," That is it. It is not necessary to explain how you were wronged at the last company you worked for or that you don't have a clue what you are doing.

Because you DO have a clue, you are in the process of getting fired up and moving forward. By not having an elaborate story or explaining in great depth the unfairness of your last boss, you open up potential chances for networking or possibly even getting positive reinforcement from unexpected outlets. Many people may be unhappy in their jobs, but they continue to go through the motions of everyday work life until something propels them to make a change. Ideally, the need for change would be recognized internally, then planned, created and executed, but getting fired can often expedite this for you.

## XI. Next Steps, Resources & Knowing When to Ask For Help

After being laid off or fired, you must have a grieving period, otherwise, you will be suppressing fragile emotions and it can be self destructive down the line. A week is a reasonable time period. Vent to trusted friends or family, engage in activities that you were unable to do because of your work constraints and do something fun.

However, do not spend a lot of money unless you have carefully calculated any severance pay, forecasted your finances and deemed okay for this spending.

After your termination, you may have follow-up communication with the human resources department in which they will offer you outsourcing services or other tools to transition employment.

**Remember: "Success is not final, failure is not fatal: it is the courage to continue that counts."**

-Winston Churchill

The number two search on the internet today is job searching. If anything proves you are not alone, this should. Granted, not everyone searching for jobs has been fired, but you are in good company.

Because this book is not meant to be a job listings book, I will not spend a lot of time and pages with listings of job agencies, I will, however, describe resourceful outlets. Even more important than job sites is to look for your next opportunity. It is important to explore options which you may never have considered as possibilities during your pre-fired days.

These outlets deserve attention, but of course, you must pay the bills. Instead of taking the first job you can find, think about the reality of making life-long changes to bring honesty and happiness to your life. There are compromises, maybe you have to take that Wal-Mart clerking job, but strive higher and continue your quest until you find something which you can live with. You deserve happiness so do not settle for anything less.

One of the best things you can do when you are in this transition phase is to stay active in a positive manner. If you need a day or two to relax, stay in bed, watch a couple movies, read a book, do it. Then, clean your house from top to bottom and organize your closets and repair anything which needs it.

Next, decide upon a fitness routine which you can easily fit into your lifestyle. For example, if your money is now tight due to your new situation, joining the trendiest gym is not your best option, but if the climate is good, try going for a brisk walk or run every morning. Get up like you would for work only get dressed and begin your workout. If you can afford some small dumbbells or resistance bands, buy those and commit to ten minutes a day only and you will feel a difference. Physical fitness lend to emotional well-being.

Then, make your lists of how you are going to move forward. You need to look at all networking contacts and let everyone know you are looking for a new opportunity. If you are single, go to a speed-dating event. You should not feel bad or less confident that you are changing jobs or careers. Tell all prospective dates that you are excited about making a change and I guarantee this will be perceived as an attractive trait. You may get a date or even a job lead and at this time, both of those can be a big boost.

The reality is that most of us may not have time to really have a relaxed approach to the job search. If you only have a months pay to bridge you from now until you are depleted again, you must move fast. Even if you have six months pay and it feels like you have enough, it will go faster than you think and finding a job could take longer than you anticipate. Also, it's a good time to make changes, but these changes, although positive in the long term, may require short-term sacrifices.

Aside from immediate job searching and networking, you can search within and think about things you have always wanted to do, but for some reason have put off. For instance, you enjoy pottery, but you have only taken one class and you recognize that you are not going to be the next best thing in the art scene. However, you notice a trend of younger people participating in this hobby. You could look at the possibility of opening a pottery studio.

You may think you don't have the money to start this business, but try to look at calculated risks, such as a small loan or partnering with someone.

If you are clearly not a risk taker and you do not want to open your own shop, maybe you could teach an art class to children. There are many possibilities and you may not have been able to see them clearly at different times, but if you keep exploring, researching and you are persistent and you can find the inner strength to value yourself and realize you do not deserve anything less than happiness, this will propel you to keep going until you find the best balance for you.

If you do have some time, look at volunteering. If you have an interest in something particular, seek out projects in those interests. For example, you really love animals, but you know you don't want to be a veterinarian or a dog breeder, but what about helping an equine non-profit organization? You could volunteer your time to assist children with disabilities to ride horses in a program of therapy.

This does not have to lead to a job, although you may be surprised to find outlets as a paid board member or recognize your strengths as a fundraiser and negotiate a role to do this, but outside that you are setting yourself up to interact with diverse persons, to make friends and to feel good about how you spend your time and energy.

Don't think you have to take this on full force and lose momentum in your job search. You can try to find an organization which can work with the time you have to offer. Even if it is just once or twice a month, you will be making yourself a vital part of the community and the reward will be great.

The SMARTER system can be useful for planning your career goals:

**S**pecific: be as clear as you can and avoid ambiguous statements.

**M**easurable: so you can see what you have achieved.

**A**chievable: provides motivation, but also keep your goals reachable.

**R**ealistic: be reasonable and avoid the realms of fantasy.

**T**imely: create timeframes for completing steps. Ask mentors for realistic time tables to complete education or begin to turn a profit in a business.

**E**mpowering: make sure your goals feel right for you and help you make the changes you want for life-work balance.

**R**eviewable: do not set your goals in concrete; be flexible.

## XII.  Know Thy Self

Logically, we know that what we do for a living does not define who we are as people. But, when you are spending the bulk of your waking hours either commuting to a job, working and thinking about something related to your job, you can feel a bit of a slave to your job, even if you really like it.

Again, let's apply the art of perspective here. We have a limited time here on earth and the idea is to fill that time with as much happiness as possible. Life is naturally challenging and it is because of this that we can compare, contrast and all the more appreciate the good times.

Understandably, one hundred percent of our time cannot be spent in leisure and avoiding anything we dislike. We must pay our taxes, do monotonous daily tasks and communicate to the relatives which annoy us.

For most of us, we must also find some type of livelihood to pay the bills. I suggest that the key to doing all of this and achieving happiness is to ***know thy self***.

The better you know yourself, the more equipped you are to make better decisions regarding your life and achieving balance within your family, your career and all you choose to take on.

I will illustrate a personal experience which demonstrates how I ignored this and I found myself enduring a chain of difficult obstacles, which could have been avoided had I listened to my inner voice more. I owned and managed a business for over four years. It was part of a very popular chain of fitness clubs for women only. But, that is not all; I started this business in a foreign country and province in which there were no existing franchises.

Not only did I take a business risk, but I took risks at every level in my personal life, my emotional well-being and although

I came out of it successfully, I paid a very high price because I ignored my inner voice and all of the screams of caution.

What I saw as an opportunity (after a period of job transition), was the chance to tackle many exciting things. What I ignored was the amount of new challenges I was trying to take on all at one time. Because separately these same things would have been manageable, but when mixed together, they became a recipe for disaster. This is like many things in life in which the key is moderation. The other key is know thy self and to know that if you cannot drink one glass of wine at a cocktail party like everyone else, for instance and you know this, then make the decision to control this by whatever method, and you can live a much more balanced life.

Speaking of balance, ironically, I had named this business I started Dolce Equilibrium, which in Italian means "sweet balance." At the time, I had had the vision of moving to the Mediterranean from a busy cosmopolitan city in the United States to begin a new life with my partner of several months, to learn a new language, to run a wellness business and to achieve "sweet balance."

This is meant to be only a chapter, not a book in itself (stay tuned for the trilogy I am writing), so I will suffice it to say that my challenge quickly turned to a source of stress and frustration which literally made me sick.

I ignored my inner voice, all of the doubts and I said to myself "I can learn a new language in the first six months, my new romance will continue and it will not be effected, according to my business plan, I will do well financially and money will not be a stress factor and, if it doesn't work out, I can always move out of this country and do something else."

None of those turned out to be true. It has taken years to learn the language(s) and perfecting the language is a constant work in progress, my relationship was absolutely put to some tough tests and I rode the hardest financial rollercoaster of my life (which, therefore, hindered my moving countries)!

I am glad to say that the business had peaks and valleys, but the exit strategy was to sell it and see it continue and that is what has happened. I can be proud of the efforts as it provided me a livelihood for over four years and the business is now in its seventh year (under other management), it was the first franchise started in Cataluña and now there are hundreds in operation or under construction.

I am also happy to say that my relationship turned into a marriage and we produced a beautiful family. And, while I am not where I want to be financially, I am on the path to achieve this, I enjoy my professional life and my day-to-day life taking in the simple pleasures and the complexities of human nature and society.

When several years of high school French did not stick, I really should have known that I was not inclined to learn languages like some. I can honestly say one of my most outstanding achievements was teaching aerobics in a foreign language that I did not know. That same week, I appeared on one of the largest radio stations in Spain to promote my business and talk about wellness. The night before, I was translating everything I would say, at first into Catalan and then, my team and I decided to go with Castilian as time was running out.

The next day, I was full of nerves and not because of public speaking as I had appeared on television and radio before and enjoyed it, but I was clearly taking on more than I should have and instead of listening to my inner self, I continued to go down the path of who I wanted to be and not who I actually was at the time.

The show turned out fine and I ended up speaking in English and my team translated it to Castilian, then the radio host spoke back in Catalan. It was the longest half hour of my life, but comedic and interesting at the same time.

Sometimes it works out, but other times it can be a disaster. I think women, particularly have this problem because we multi-task by nature and we also give birth to children. Men, on the other hand, tend to be terrible at multi-tasking and have no potential for the later.

Women put added pressure on themselves due often to the ticking clock or the desire to have it all. I think women can "have it all," but maybe not all at once. I know my reasons for having children later in life was because I wanted to do so many things professionally and personally. I felt that I would not be able to take career risks or travel for pleasure as much with children. I now have many more options in my professional life, which allow me to shift my priorities to raising a family.

I also know many families who started having children very young and have had much success and either later in life pursued other interests or decided the contentment with more focus on family was preferred.

I do not, however, know many women who have had the family, the career, personal and relationship balance and have done it all successfully, without something having to suffer. We all must make sacrifices at different times in our lives and the better you know your own capacity and make choices that follow this honesty, the happier you will ultimately be in achieving that sweet balance.

Although there is no substitute for life experience, if you are open to external opinions, tools (Getting Fired Up!) or proactive by nature, you can greatly benefit by making changes, accordingly.

We all hear things from people with experience such as "Your wedding will go so fast, you won't remember much," "Divorce is the worst emotional roller coaster," "You don't know what it is like to be a parent until you have your own family." All of the statements are repeated over and over again because people with life experience try to lend advice to others who have not yet experienced the aforementioned.

What happens is that these statements go in one ear and out the other until a person has actually experienced things firsthand at which point he or she recalls hearing these statements and it all becomes relevant.

We all go through life stages contingent upon educational, family and work experiences. In our twenties we are trying to be relevant and find our path. The drive and ambition is somewhat wasted on the youth as the life experience has not yet shaped our development.

Our thirties and forties can be thriving times for our professional lives, but typically family responsibilities impact these years.

In the fifties and sixties, professional lives can often peak; however, with job market volatility professional careers can end suddenly as well.

With life, family, job transitions occurring later in life, many are working into their sixties and seventies.

My grandfather, a successful orthopaedic surgeon peaked in his career in his sixties and is currently 83 years old. He has an amazing professional life that continues to thrive, although he is quite exceptional and this is not attainable for most of us.

When job loss hits, it can seem like the most crushing blow in the world until you or your loved one is faced with a serious or life threatening illness.

Often the variables that influence life and work change cannot be controlled like we would want them to be, but we can control our reactions to this change.

The movie *Under the Tuscan* sun really dramatizes how our dreams sometimes do come true, but often evolve differently than we had envisioned.

The importance in understanding this is that if you let yourself be compared to others with regard to status, profession, marital status, etc., it will be impossible to be authentically happy.

Everyone has different goals, time tables and capacity for change.

## EIGHT WAYS TO STOP PROCRASTINATING NOW

What can you do to accomplish more of what you want to do? Here are some immediate suggestions:

1. **Choose the easiest place to start**

   You don't always have to start at the beginning. If that first step seems the hardest, start with another part of the project instead.

2. **Fix your workspace**

   If your set-up is simply not convenient, it will definitely hold you back.

3. **Work from your to-do list**

   Tackle the more difficult tasks during your prime time.

4. **Be realistic about what you can do**

   Procrastinators often have an unrealistic sense of time; you may have the feeling that a project will take forever or that you have "plenty of time." The more realistic you become, the less likely you'll be to procrastinate.

5. **Use the minutes available to you**

   Realize even five minutes is enough time to get something done. One or two phone calls or more can be returned in that time.

6. **Reward yourself**

   After you meet small deadlines, promise yourself a small treat. When the entire project is completed, think on a little grander scale.

7. **Create more time**

   If it seems like there really is no time, carve out a half hour or so from your existing schedule. If you really want to take up jogging, try getting up a half hour earlier each day (or on weekends). If you want to do it, you'll find the time.

8. **Get started**

The hardest part is getting started. Once you're in motion, it will be easier to keep going. You may well find that it isn't as bad as you expected, and once you're involved, you've overcome the highest hurdle.

## XIII. Ego & You Are Not Your Job

We are constantly judging others and being judged. After living in Europe for many years, I made some interesting discoveries of human nature and I would like to challenge you to try something at the next cocktail party or social outing you attend. Try to introduce yourself to other persons and restrain from asking what that person does for a living and stop yourself from answering questions about what you do for a living. Seemingly easy, but in American culture, this is the second most frequently asked information in a first meeting, just after a persons´ name.

I have noticed in Europe, this is not the case at all. After an initial introduction, the conversation will go in many directions, but not directly to the question of livelihood. It would seem indelicate and odd if asked. This is not to say that if you are in a work setting, meeting other contemporaries in your industry, that this would play out as such, that is a situation in which it is unavoidable due to the immediate relevancy.

Why is this so? In Spain, for instance, the work force is comprised of many self-employed, small business owners, along with people who work in all size businesses which are not much different than many regions of the world you might say.

However, in Spain, there are a large amount of family owned businesses or "mom & pop shops" and while many people run a very modest bar or work in a street front shop the size of my former walk-in closet, they are perfectly happy doing what they do and it was known to them that when the time came, they would be working in the family business.

While they work in this business, it may not have been something they dreamed of doing, but it is quite possible that many are happy to continue this family business and keep this as their main source of income because it is suitable to their way of life.

When you speak to these people, they do not think of themselves as "shop worker" or "bar worker," they simply see that as only one aspect of their lives. This could explain the limited shop hours (opening at 10am and most close mid-day from 1pm until 5pm to return and work 5-8pm). Further, on Sundays most shops are all closed because it has typically been the day for families to gather for the mid-day meal when they go to the family home and stay until late at night.

Whatever the reason, I think it has to do with perspective. The popular phrase "Work to Live, Not Live to Work," really seems to reflect in the Europeans attitudes towards the importance of a job in a persons' life.

In American popular culture, the significance placed on external materials or roles is huge. This is not to say that Europeans do not pass judgement when a person pulls up in the latest Mercedes May bach because I have seen the jaws drop, but rather emphasis seems to be placed differently in different societies and while it's great to appreciate the material things in life or respect someone for their position in a company or in the government or have admiration for a musical talent, these are *roles* and not the entire person.

Unfortunately, we are judgemental in the wrong ways and if you meet a garbage collector who is filling a vital community role, you may not give the same level of respect to that person as you would to the CEO of a large fortune 500 company, who commands power and wealth. But, what if that company was Enron?

And, if you know you should not judge others so harshly, then why do we judge ourselves in such a destructive manner?

You got fired, it's not such a devastating event when you look at global affairs. I know, it *feels* like it is at the time. But, if you can get outside yourself for a moment and know that you will move forward in your life and the best has yet to come, you can take great comfort in knowing that you are not alone, you have resources to help guide you and you will get through this.

Throwing yourself into a self exploration project can help to take the focus off the feelings of loss from not having a job. In most cases, you will need to update your resume, so take this opportunity to take it a step further by redefining your professional self on paper.

Once you have achieved this, you can begin to launch your personal public relations campaign. By doing this, you can gain exposure which might lead to broadening your professional profile. It can also keep you socializing, networking and active so that you can feel empowered in your professional and personal development.

Many people site the lack of control as the main source of stress after losing a job and when searching for a job. While you cannot control the availability of the job you want, you can control many factors that can help you achieve success in the job searching process.

For example, job searching is very much a numbers game, like many sales roles. The more your resume is circulated, the more you attend job fairs, network and continually look for places to highlight your professional experience, the more likely you are to gain employment.

The public relations campaign can be fun and it basically entails doing anything and everything you can think of to get your resumé in the hands of decision makers. You do not always know who the decision makers are, so be ready at all times. When you attend church, take a moment to ask for support in your job search. The person sitting next to you may be a recruiter or know someone else who is able to make an introduction.

Be creative and have fun with it. Throw a cupcake party and have all of your guests leave with a cupcake and your email address to pass along to potential employers. Organize a golf game to network. Most jobs are not advertised and it's

88

important to make everyone aware that you are looking for a job and you would appreciate their assistance.

Not only does this PR campaign get you in control and on the path to success, but it leaves less time for negative thoughts to creep in leaving you paralyzed in fear or self doubt.

You have probably heard before that it is easier to get a job when you already have one. This is, statistically speaking, true and those who are pursuing new opportunities while working do have more control.

Within the public relations realm, perception is everything. I am a big proponent of creating an image and promoting it to others while utilizing calculated methods. However, there is a clear distinction between creating an image that you would like to promote and falsifying information. At no point, should one ever be deceitful in the personal public relations campaign to bring professional success.

For obvious reasons of character, a person would not want this to reflect negatively on them as a person. Secondly, if you are hired into a company on false pretences and later called out, you can be terminated and face worse consequences.

So, when I allude to promotion of assets and the playing down of select past experience, I intend for this to be within a context of truth and honesty, but a way to portray you in the best light.

# XIV. CASE STUDIES

Larry Stybel

Some people become entrepreneurs because it was their passion for years. Others are thrust into it because there is no choice. I was in the latter category and it was the best thing that ever happened to me.

I was working for an organization and was fired. The fact that I was fired was not astonishing. I knew it wasn't a good fit. But the way in which I was fired was so demoralizing I was depressed for nearly a year.

I got a job to tide me through. But the way in which I had been fired really bothered me. Eventually I was accepted into the doctoral program in organization behavior at Harvard University and wrote my doctoral thesis on how employees are fired and how does the way in which the firing get conducted impact the organization. My thesis was a way to intellectually comprehend what had emotionally torn me apart.

After graduation, I started an executive outplacement company called Stybel Peabody Lincolnshire. We are based in Boston and have offices in 25 countries and 40 U.S. cities. We are retained by companies to work with executives to help them with their careers and we work with our client companies to make sure that nothing ever happens to these employees that happened to me.

We have been in business for nearly 30 years.

Thanks to my firing I have made a good living, helped others who have been fired, and am one of the few people I know who has made a living off his doctoral thesis.

Leanna Adams

What are the top things you look for in employment (pay,benefits,etc)? I look for pay and hours of work. I write in my free time, so I'm interested in a job where I am not worked around the clock. If that's the case, I want to be well compensated for it.

What has been the most frustrating part of being laid off or fired (feelings of being inadequate, income, etc.)? The most frustrating part is to not know when it will end and the feelings of embarrassment every time I tell friends that I'm out of work.

Have you made a jump into starting your own business or returning to school, etc? I have started my own freelance writing business, but at this stage, I'll take the work I can get even if that means doing some data entry.

How many hours a week do you spend searching for work? I spend about 2 hours a week searching for fulltime jobs and about 5 hours a week searching for freelance work.

What is your process? (Internet, networking, newspaper) I use the internet and my personal network.

Do you think finding a job is harder now than when you first started working or is it different as you are at a different age, experience level, etc.? I think it is harder for me now that the economy is in the dumps. Also, with my experience, my expected pay rate has gone up from when I first entered the workforce and I am more specialized which probably also makes it tougher.

Have you decided to return to something you did and had passion for but never realized success (music career, etc)? No.

Have you taken part time or volunteer jobs while you continue to search? No.

Are you depressed or do you stay positive? I oscillate between feelings like I'm making my business work to feeling depressed that I'm not where I want to be financially.

What support systems do you have in place (do you have a spouse with ability to pay bills, etc while you search, do you go to internet blogs for motivation)? I have a supportive husband, family and friends. Unfortunately, I do not have a financial support – my husband's pay cannot solely pay our bills.

Has this experience been a blessing in disguise? I hope so! I would love to look back in six months or a year or even three years and say, "Getting laid off was the best thing that's ever happened to me!"

Have you had to change your standard of living while job searching or use your savings? I've had to change my standard of living. I DO NOT eat out nearly as much as I used to, which means I grocery shop and plan out meals more. This has surprisingly been a highlight of being laid off. I'm enjoying baking and cooking for my husband and myself.

Were you happy with your severance package or did you think you were treated unfairly upon exit (financially)? I did not receive severance or notice. I was very unhappy about this. While I had seen small signs that the company might not make it, that abrupt ending was no less difficult for me.

Was the firing or lay off unexpected or were there red flags in the lead up? There were small red flags, little comments and the fact that some of our clients left us due to monetary issues in the economy.

Is it hard to relate to the government bailout of AIG and big corporations when you, as an individual, are suffering with no golden parachute? Or do you agree with the bailout to prevent more persons unemployed to compete with in the job search? At first, I was outraged about the bailout, but I do see that there is probably not another way to stabilize our economy and keep more layoffs at bay.

Have you adjusted your goals (now feel you can accept less money to do something you enjoy or realized you must make more money to get security for future situations)? I now realize that I must make more money in order to have the standard of living that I want and make the savings that my family needs for the future.

Have you started a business on the side while you job search? Do you think you can make a viable income or is it something to do in a hobby capacity and bring in some extra money? I have started a business and I think with time it can become viable income, but it is not yet.

Michael Levy, Career HP Employee

Number of years in workforce & age started to work (if you started working summer jobs at 15, but then went to college and resumed working then, count total years, but make note):

I have roughly 25 years in the workforce. I started working a summer job at 14. I continued part time through college. Then, I worked full-time through most of my 20's, sometimes 2 jobs. I took 8 years off, collectively, while returning to college and raising a family. I am 42 years old.

Number of jobs you have been fired or laid off from: Just laid-off from 2.

Are you in specific industry (engineering, legal, etc.)? Multi-media (broadcasting) and Information Technology

Are you specialized (marketing, sales)? In IT I concentrated in Help Desk Support.

What are the top things you look for in employment (pay, benefits, etc)?

Location, Pay, Benefits, pertaining vacation, perks.

What has been the most frustrating part of being laid off or fired (feelings of being inadequate, income, etc.)?

The most frustrating part has been the loss of income. This necessitated pulling my kids out of their afterschool care program.

Have you made a jump into starting your own business or returning to school, etc?

I have taken this opportunity to go back to doing work that I loved and miss. So I am starting my own business.

How many hours a week do you spend searching for work?

Normally, 8-10.

What is your process? (Internet, networking, newspaper)

I mostly utilize the Internet as well as some networking and newspapers.

Do you think finding a job is harder now than when you first started working or do you think it different as you are at a different age, experience level, etc.?

I have found both situations share some common qualities. When you are first starting out your lack of experience is the barrier, even to entry level positions. When you have experience oftentimes companies do want your skills but do not want to pay the market rate. They want to pay you a near to entry level salary.

Have you decided to return to something you did and had passion for but never realized success (music career, etc)?

Yes, in a way. I felt I was successful but, not at the level I intended because I never gave it a chance nor did I invest the effort to expose myself to more opportunities in the field of broadcasting.

Have you taken part time or volunteer jobs while you continue to search?

I am not as much searching for employment at this time as much as I am building my business. I have always found time to volunteer and will always continue to do so regardless of my career situation.

Are you depressed or do you stay positive?
I am positive, although it is not always easy to maintain.

What support systems do you have in place (do you have a spouse with ability to pay bills, etc while you search, do you go to internet blogs for motivation)?
My spouse's income can sustain us. It does need to stretch quite a bit but we can manage for the time being.

Has this experience been a blessing in disguise?
Yes, it absolutely has. I believe that I would not have been able to make a career change otherwise.

Have you had to change your standard of living while job searching or use your savings? No. we can pay our bills. We just need to plan our expenses a little more carefully.

Were you happy with your severance package or did you think you were treated unfairly upon exit (financially)?

I did not receive any severance. I am collecting unemployment insurance.

Was the firing or lay off unexpected or were there red flags in the lead up?

It was not unexpected. There were a number of corporate red flags such as new staff having their probation periods extended. In my case I recognized that there was too much staff in my department for the workload. In addition, while I was on a vacation my shift was not covered by other staff.

Do you have legal action pending against former employer? No.

Is it hard to relate to the government bailout of AIG and big corporations when you, as an individual, are suffering with no golden parachute? Or do you agree with the bailout to prevent more persons unemployed to compete with in the job search?

While I understand the reasoning behind the bailout intention, I do find it hard to relate. Part of this has to do with the very nature of the financial world of business. I do find it difficult to understand how financial advisors can in one turn say that the market is self-correcting and then in the next moment say that if the government does nothing it will all collapse. In this instance there are still thousands of financial workers who will receive major bonuses this year. It is hard to wrap your head around that...and in a way it is unfair. I do believe that the US needs to protect its financial stability in the foreign markets. But I also feel that the average guy is the one that bears the brunt.

Have you adjusted your goals (now feel you can accept less money to do something you enjoy or realized you must make more money to get security for future situations)?

At this stage in my life the reality is that I do need to make more money in order to have a stable financial future. Certain expenses remain constant even when others lessen.

Have you started a business on the side while you job search? Do you think you can make a viable income or is it something to do in a hobby capacity and bring in some extra money?

For now I can rely on my weekly unemployment insurance while my business gets off the ground. At some I know I can always bring in extra income if absolutely necessary.

Are you targeting other professions to get into which may have more stability?

In a way I am. Working as a voice-over actor appears to be a stable career...not so much for the daily "job". Look at this from the other perspective. There will always be products to sell; audio books to record, voice on hold greetings, etc. The work is always out there.

Have you decided to do something completely different now (move countries, start a family, travel)?

More travelling would be great...but first I need more money to able to do so.

The following is an article by Christine Steele of The Daily Reporter-Herald published on 6/26/2005 about Michael and I thought I would share it as it describes life after layoffs.

Friday the 13th was the best day of Michael Levy's life.

That September 2002 day was when he got his walking papers from Hewlett-Packard.

Levy, a 30-year employee with the company, had been working there since high school. He was 48 years old two years shy of being able to take advantage of the company's early retirement plan. But he wasn't bitter.

"It was unfortunate," he said. "But my dad told me growing up not to rely on Social Security or your company to take care of you, and I listened to that."

Levy had put away some savings and bought some investment property, but still, he said, the separation was scary.

With the job market as tight as it was in Northern Colorado, Levy said he looked around for two months and considered moving out of state for a job. But with two teenage daughters in school and a wife who was a teacher in the community, Levy said he was reluctant to uproot his family after seven years here.

Having previously lived in San Francisco and Bristol, England, when Levy was with Hewlett-Packard, the family had done some traveling, but Levy said they liked Northern Colorado and wanted to stay. That is when he realized he needed to make something happen himself.

With Agilent's recent announcement of another round of layoffs, this may be good advice to those joining the ranks of the recently unemployed.

While Levy said he was never bitter about being let go, he understands being laid off can elicit feelings of anger and bitterness. He says you have to limit the time you spend dwelling on that.

"I have never felt that a company is obligated to take care of me in any respect," he said.

"I never had the expectation that they owed me. They never told me that it was a job for life. It was for as long as they had a need for that job."

Levy's positive attitude and enthusiasm for his new projects might be part of the driving force behind his successes.

Starting with Levy Consulting, he has since launched two more companies, NorthernColoradoRentals.com, an online database of available rental real estate in the area, and HOA-Records.com, a online data storage site for homeowner association records. He is now running a fourth.

The newest company, RealGIS, offers virtual tours of real estate property in Northern Colorado. The company was founded by Ron Brush, president of New Century Software.

Brush, started New Century, a GIS consulting firm for the oil and gas industry 11 years ago, said he always wanted to start another company but hasn't had the time. By networking through the Fort Collins High-Tech Network, Brush met Bill Dieterich, who put him in touch with Levy and Bill Carson. Both had the skills and experience to help Brush launch the new company.

The right people are the key, Brush said. While having the right idea might put you a little way down the road, he said, success really comes down to the people.

"There are people waiting for jobs to come along, and others are out there trying to make something happen," he said. "I hear a lot of people complaining there are no jobs, but there are opportunities."

Levy is one who has seen these opportunities. While there might be competitors for his businesses, he said, that just tells him there is a market for what he is doing. "It's energizing," he said. "My motivation is in part the frustration I see, but part of it is fun, to have an idea about something and see it come together."

Looking back, Levy said he would never go back. Getting laid off gave him the opportunity to do something he was "too risk-adverse" to do.

"What I learned at Hewlett-Packard was the basic skills and the skills to learn," he said. "If I want a big company now, I guess I'll have to create my own.

Michael Levy, a former Hewlett-Packard employee, shows off a virtual real estate tour on his laptop while in his Fort Collins office Wednesday. Levy helped launch the company Real GIS, which specializes in virtual tours for real estate.

How and why did I get into being an Entrepreneur?

Well I always joke with my friends and say that Friday the 13$^{th}$ of September 2002 was the luckiest day of my life – because that was the day I was laid off from the Hewlett-Packard Company after 25+ years working for them. Up to that point in time I always wanted to try my hand at starting my own company but with a nice paying job and benefits it was hard to leave HP. Then I got that opportunity when I was laid off. At first it was very difficult. It was scary and a bit depressing because I started by trying to find another job working for another company. But that didn't lead to anything I was interested in doing. Then after trying to find a job for several months I decided, why not try what I've always wanted to do – start my own company! Within the first 2 years after being laid off I actually started 2 companies: a software & technology consulting company AND a rental listing website business in Northern Colorado called NorthernColoradoRentals.com.

What were some of my greatest challenges & obstacles with my rental listing website business?

First, I had to stop feeling sorry for myself – and look at the current circumstances as a VERY POSITIVE, EXCITING, and CHALLENGING new opportunity. The next challenge was putting together a compelling vision and business plan – and figuring out what our KEY COMPETITIVE DIFFERENTIATION was going to be – we eventually settled on it being "Providing UNCOMPROMISING Customer

Service & Support". Our next challenge was dealing with all the EMAIL issues we ran into. The website is essentially a self-service website and we do most communications with our customer using e-mail. The 2 biggest problems were:

1. Email "Scammers" – people typically from countries like Nigeria pretending to be "interested renters"

2. SPAM related email issues

And the other hurdle was figuring out how to deal with competitors that tried to come into our market space. Turns out our decision to make Customer Service & Support a key differentiator was a really good decision – because it worked to keep competition from stealing market share – because our customers are so happy with our service they really have no reason to even consider switching to any of our competitors.

Do I consider that business to be a success? If so, why was it considered a success?

I think it has been pretty successful. When we started out we had 2 key financial objectives that most entrepreneurs care about:

1. Become cash flow positive as quickly as possible, and we did that in our first month of operation

2. And the second was our goal to recoup our initial investment – our goal was to do that in about 12 months, and we actually were able to recoup our complete initial investment in half that time, about 6 months.

What were my keys to success? What were the critical success factors?

I think there were a few primary keys to our success:

1. Most importantly, stay focused on the key elements that would lead to making the business successful.

2. The $2^{nd}$ is probably our decision to make our #1 priority be an unwavering focus on Customer Service & Customer Satisfaction. When we first went in to full operation,

I remember when I'd wake up every morning, I'd go downstairs in my home office, and hope that there would be emails or phone calls from upset customers, because I knew that I could easily turn an unhappy customer into a very satisfied customer in say, maybe, less than 5 minutes – and then that customer would probably be a customer for life and tell 10-100 of his/her friends about us.

3. The 3$^{rd}$ key to our success is probably creating a very easy to explain and understand VALUE PROPOSITION for our customers. We made it very simple:

We were going to be 1/10$^{th}$ the cost at least 5 times more effective than any other alternative form of advertising.

We would probably be setting up the entire business from the very beginning to make sure we could easily track metrics and statistics on a daily, weekly, monthly, and annual basis. For example, we were able to easily track the effectiveness of where we spent our own advertising dollars to promote our website business. So, we know exactly how much it costs to get a new customer by advertising say on the backs of city bus benches, versus advertising in a newspaper, versus say, buying advertising using Google Ad words online. This has proven to be very useful to us when we need to make key business & financial investment decisions.

When advising other new startups in Northern Colorado – what do I find are their biggest challenges?

Well it certainly is not easy for some of these new startups trying to get their business off the ground – and what is the commonly known statistic? The fact that only 1 in 10 new startups will end up being successful is a harsh one. A key challenge for many of them is trying to get Angel or VC funding and in order to do that – they need to figure out how to build a successful **business team** that consists preferably of individuals that have a good track record of previously starting other successful startup companies. Another key challenge for many of them is figuring how to market and sell their great idea, service, or product. Many come from a more technical or product development backgrounds and they need quite a bit of help with the **sales and marketing functions**.

Have I had any failed startups?

YES. I tried to take NorthernColoradoRentals.com NATIONAL rather than just keeping it focused on Northern Colorado. I formed a company, USAPropertyRentals.com, but I wasn't able to get any traction with that business. Turns out the competition was already pretty entrenched for the national rental websites and I wasn't really able to overcome that. But I learned a lot from the experience, and many say that you become a much better entrepreneur if you've had at least one failure – so now I now have my ONE failure and so I don't need any more of those.

What is my newest startup endeavor?

I'm starting an Advertising Services business for local advertisers and for high volume website owners here in Northern Colorado. My partner and I are **REALLY** excited about this new venture and it'll be called NoCoAds.com – so everyone will have to keep an eye out for that new venture

116

coming online in the next few months. The startup costs will be under $1K, and it will be highly profitable.

## XV. WORKSHEET FOR PLANNING

# WORKSHEET FOR PLANNING

# WORKSHEET FOR PLANNING

# WORKSHEET FOR PLANNING

# WORKSHEET FOR PLANNING

# WORKSHEET FOR PLANNING

# WORKSHEET FOR PLANNING

# WORKSHEET FOR PLANNING

WORKSHEET FOR PLANNING

# WORKSHEET FOR PLANNING

## XVI. Daily Practice of Control & Self-Discipline

It would be wonderful if someone could just make a call and get you that dream job you have been wanting or if there was a magic pill you could take to have that perfectly toned body, but as we know these things require self-control and discipline. This is not anything you do not already know.

However, I think where most people go wrong is that they underestimate the power of the mind. For instance, if your thoughts are always negative about yourself or other people, you are emitting negative energy into the universe whether you open your mouth of not.

The pro-active thing to do would be to emit positive thoughts and energy and this should be your goal. But, at the very least try to be aware of the negative dialogue which takes place in your mind on a daily basis. I suggest if you could eliminate or decrease this, you will benefit immensely.

One exercise to try for this is to be very aware of the Olympic games of your mind. For two days, keep a notepad and pen handy and every time you catch yourself thinking something negative about yourself or someone else or situations in general, write it down. At the end of the two days, look at the list and you will probably realize the damaging energy you have been throwing out to the universe. This energy finds its' way back to you in ways you may or may not be conscious of.

Of course, this tactic applies to every facet of your life, not just your job. These facets are all inter-related; none of them are mutually exclusive. The more you can strike a balance, the healthier and happier you will be in life.

Another thing which is very important in making changes in life, whether it be your diet, exercise or professional transition, is to set realistic goals. Do not set the goal to join a gym and workout everyday for the next year; do not tell yourself that if you do not have a new job by the end of the month, you are worthless.

A constant evaluation needs to be done and adjustments made, accordingly, but if you set goals too high, you are setting yourself up for unneeded failure. Instead, set the goal to go walking once a week and then, twice a week, then, add free weights – you are seeing the pattern.

Target ten companies a day to approach in person or in writing for a job; research technical schools and allow time to compile a list. You are much more likely to begin to feel good about the successes from small changes.

XVII. Keep Clarity in Your Priorities & Launch a Personal Public Relations Campaign

If you have recently experienced job loss, but you have actively participated in a plan to move forward, sometimes you can lose sight of your longer term goals in the everyday circus of life.

For instance, you are taking some night classes to become a realtor, but you must pay your current bills so you take a temporary job as an administrative assistant and that pays the current bills, but you know you must now raise some capital to infuse your real estate business in six months. So, you take a weekend job waiting tables. Three months into working very hard, you get discouraged as the last table you waited on was rude to you and left you no tip, the temporary job may be ending soon and you are just feeling depleted.

Mental exercises of envisioning yourself putting up a real estate sign with your name on it and signing a contract for your first commissions can keep you going long enough to keep you outside of your comfort zone reaching further and striving higher.

How many times do we introduce and repeat self-defeating words in our minds? Telling ourselves that we can't do it or I won't be successful. The mind is a muscle and it is vital to do positive workouts daily. It may be hard to eliminate the negative thoughts completely, but we must put up a good fight by provoking positive images more often than not.

This can be done through daily planned meditation or by working into your life in a more permanent manner in which you stop negativity in its tracks as it arises. Either way, recognize that you must fight to keep your mind clear.

Communication is important, not only for raising your profile, but to keep your sanity. Sometimes when you are forced out of an office environment, you can feel isolated. This isolation breeds insecurity and now is when you need your highest levels of self-confidence to shine through.

Even if you propel yourself into social environments, it will be helpful to give your perspective and maintain balance. With approaching interviews, you want to be readily available to talk about yourself and your professional experiences. If you stay active socially, you will be constantly rehearsing this part of your interview. Obviously, you will tweak it for the professional side, but it will help you to think on your feet and adapt quickly.

Your weekly bible study class may present an opportunity to speak on a topic – take it! The more experience you can gain with public speaking, the more comfortable you will be when you do get those interviews.

Everyone operates differently, so find the best system for you and incorporate it into your new schedule. For instance, I am a "list person" and I like the feeling of making a list and at the end of the day or week checking off all I have accomplished. This not only makes me feel like I am making progress, it forces me to evaluate how I am spending my time and redistribute efforts if needed.

Because you are now out of a "9 to 5" schedule, it is important that you add structure to your new routine, or you will waste precious time and opportunity in finding the next best thing for yourself.

The schedule brings clarity to your goals. If you need a support system, try to wedge some accountability into your day. For example, schedule appointments with career counsellors or resume advisors to help keep you on track. Even if you have been in the workforce many years, this is good to do since resume styles change and it is a competitive market which requires you to constantly be on top of your game.

Time is really a variable we have allowed to be the focus in our lives. I think that it is highly important to live in the present and learn from the past, but avoid regret or emotion based on past events.

To some extent, it is necessary to plan for the near future and more distant future, but we do not live for tomorrow or we lose our today. So, to help achieve goals, develop daily, weekly, monthly and yearly (out 1-3yrs) plans. Situations can change so quickly, so realize adaptability is the key to thriving in this fast paced modern world.

XVIII. The Plan: 1 Month, 6 Months, 1 Year, 3 Years

INSERT PLAN:

INSERT PLAN:

INSERT PLAN:

INSERT PLAN:

INSERT PLAN:

INSERT PLAN:

INSERT PLAN:

INSERT PLAN:

INSERT PLAN:

INSERT PLAN:

INSERT PLAN:

INSERT PLAN:

INSERT PLAN:

## XIX.   Unexpected Detours

As you now have a plan, it is important to understand that everything can change in one day as you may have experienced if you were recently fired. Recognize the things you have control over and the things you do not and act accordingly.

It sounds amazingly simple, but it requires practice. For instance, you may think you are a perfect match for a job, but you never get a call from the hiring company, you must recognize that this is outside your control and if that is the case, you cannot worry about it. Just navigate the best you can.

You may have just started a new job in which requires 90% travel and is very high pressure and you suddenly realize that you are pregnant with twins!

Don´t loose momentum, just adapt as quickly as possible and you may find things have a way of working out for the better.

Life is not a clear path, so recognizing the bumps in the road as being neither positive nor negative, frees you to navigate your best route. Keep your emotions in check when navigating road bumps so that you can keep moving forward. For instance, if you know that you must get less sleep and drastically cut back your expenses in order to start your new business, it's important to focus on the positive feelings the end goal will bring and not dwell in the pain and hardship along the path.

Your friends may be out enjoying a good time shopping or on the latest vacation, but your reward will be your achievement, so do not fall into the trap of feeling that you are missing out.

The price for instant gratification can be high. Don't let it detour your determination to meet your goals.

## XX.  Re-Evaluate

The grass is always greener. Again, this plays to our perception and how we use it. If you work for a company and you are imprisoned by a cubicle or rigid office hours and departmental demands, you may look at your business owner friends with much envy.

They seem to be able to go to the in the middle of the day, sleep late and take vacations whenever they please. As a business owner, I implore you to look more closely. In other words, if finances get tight, they must take loans to meet payroll or endure intense stress for months awaiting inventory that is delayed.

And, I assure you, like the single friend looking to her married friends and thinking they have it made and vice-versa, it is natural to think that others have it better than you do.

Why is this important to analyze? It is of the utmost importance to understand this when you are sitting in your cubicle and thinking how life would be much easier and better if only you owned your own business.

This is not to discourage anyone from starting a business, quite the contrary, but do not enter into it with the mindset that it will end your unhappiness. It might turn out to be all you hoped for, but you may go through some difficult times before you realize this success.

If you are competitive by nature, you understand the importance of getting psyched up before a competitive game. This technique works well when transitioning from the corporate world to self-employment or vice-versa.

The due diligence process can also help to avoid unexpected detours. While this is done formally with the purchase of a franchise or other business, I suggest those choosing a professional path do it thoroughly as well. For instance, if you have been fired or laid off and want to become a nurse as you know high paying jobs exist and it's something you have always wanted to do, you must do your homework.

Talk to nurses and ask them about their experiences. Was it what they expected after they completed the education? Possibly you are expecting 9 to 5 hours and realize that you must be prepared for 12 hour shifts. Investing time and money into education is just as significant, if not more, than funnelling money into buying a new business.

Ironically, when I owed one of my fitness businesses, I was the most unfit person you have met. I opened the first American franchise, Curves for Women, a 30 minutes workout in 2001. I was in a foreign country, with a man I had known less than a year. I was not fluent in Spanish, let alone Catalan. I was not trained in aerobics, fitness nor was I leading a healthy lifestyle. I did the minimal training in order to acquire my franchise. I had just undergone a very devastating personal loss in the United States. Two weeks later, I was in training for a fitness franchise and two weeks after that, I closed on two houses, sold two cars and flew to a foreign country. I arrived in said country and I immediately changed from social smoker to chain smoker. I underwent extreme stress due to finances and so many life changes.

I would wait for a train or go behind my gym to smoke a cigarette. When I would do sales for a new member, I would shun them if they indicated they smoked.

Because I was not married at the time and I was not a mother, I could not relate to women with children. I ranked them as an inconvenient member as their cancel rate was always much higher than the single woman. Little did I realize then that they were the most valuable members.

When you are in a foreign country for a few months or even a year, you do not have truly the experience.

Once you are in a country foreign to you after ten years, you may think you would capture the customs, the language, and demeanor. For me, it was no different than many of my expat friends or acquaintances. It weighs on you more heavily, year after year.

It is more the culture than the language.

When you realize owning a business, marriage, having kids or aging are not easy things. Add the difficulty in doing these things in a foreign country and you would think my counterparts were shear geniuses or the luckiest people on earth.

What I said to my daughter when she was three years old was "you don't know until you go," it seems to speak volumes. It was meant at bedtime. In order to say, if you are tired, you will go to sleep, if you are not you wont go, but if you know, you go." And that is how it is in life, if you know, you go....if you don't know, you don't go.

We want to be go-getters in life. If you don't rake a risk or chance, you don't grow in character or in any materialistic way. Stagnation does nobody any good.

It is important to understand definitively where you want to you in life, otherwise, you cannot define your path.

If you do not define a clear path, you will not succeed. You will slap around until you arrive at your unknown destination and you will go from there.

That is not the way you want to go through life. You want to map your future and define your path. Obviously, along the way, there are factors that can derail you or slow you down; the sign of a strong person is to navigate the path and not let the small things slow you down.

If you are constantly avoiding the grander things life has to offer you, you will settle for almost anything.

If you constantly push yourself outside your comfort zone, you will go beyond any restrictions you have set on yourself.

Realize as early as possible that we live in a material world and the limitations are endless, regardless of beauty, socio-economic status, intelligence, etc. This has been proven over and over again from rags to riches stories from ordinary people to celebrities. Oprah Winfrey came from a social class of nothing and became one of the most powerful women in the world.

What separates you from her? You can no longer use social class, etc for an excuse not to succeed. You may feel like the biggest loser in the world because you have not graduated from college or you lost your job.

It is nothing. That is a material presence that actually has nothing to do with reality. It is only the material world and you have to put your faith in more than a false sense of things.

The REALITY is what YOU perceive. This is shown to be more evident when you analyze the perception of personal beliefs in self worth. What do you think of yourself? You are a fake? You are worthless? You are fat and stupid? Then, you are. I am not here for "tough love," but mind over matter is more powerful than any self help book you read.

If you believe it, it is so. If you really think you are fat or stupid, you need to take steps to change this. You need to increase your studies and realize academic success at whatever level is appropriate. It you believe you are fat and it is affecting your performance in the workplace or personally; you must change this. You must lose weight. What? Did you think as an empowering woman, I was going to tell you to move beyond that feeling? NO. If you feel you are fat, lose weight. If you are ninety pounds, with an eating disorder, than you need to seek help in another way. But, if you cannot fit into clothes the way you wish, then you SHOULD take on an extreme program to change your situation.

If you are not happy with yourself, it is hard to go into a job interview to convince someone else that you are a capable person fro the position in which you are interviewing.

Make no mistake about it physical appearance is important and presentation in any job is relevant. It may make us uncomfortable, but this is the way life is and we must play by the games of the material world we live in.

We must take responsibility for our actions in work or in our personal lives. Do not make the mistake that either of these is of more importance than the other. You recognize the feelings you have w hen either component is out of balance, so it is important to continually access, re-access and change the dynamic of work, personal and family.

You must make compromises in each facet of your life at all times. There is no easy solution.

The hardest part of writing this book is the level of honesty that I must come to. It does no good to share experience, feelings and advice if it is not authentic. At the same time, when it comes from a place of authenticity, it breeds an awareness that must be dealt with.

The goal is to embrace our material world and hardships and moves forward with confidence and a sense of well being.

It is not easy to admit that you are failing at what you spend ninety percent of your time at. Whether you are a man or a woman the roles may be different. Women, who are mothers, do not get down-sized or fired. Well, not in the traditional sense. But, you are missing the mark if you think that you cannot be replaced in any capacity.

Even the ideal employee gets fired! These things happen everyday. Is it right or fair? No, absolutely not!

You cannot trust your employer to act in your best interest. So, whatever the dynamic when you are hired, the only thing you can guarantee and count on is that the dynamic will change. Now, this may sound pessimistic and I do not encourage you to think of the most negative outcome occurring at all times, but I urge you to recognize the statistics and do not believe you are different.

Most businesses fail within the first two years; divorce rates are beyond 55%...this is fact, not fiction.

If you think you can put your faith and trust in an employer or a boss you are wrong and need tough love right now. What if you could never have any of the above? Could you be all right?

Even if you have a large company to provide a check, you need a plan "B." You need a balanced family life. If you have the "perfect" husband and children which you adore and love, you need some balance somehow, somewhere.

These statements are nothing new. Do not think you are different or better than the mass population. Understand the things that can separate you from these statistics. For example, a strong belief in GOD or a higher power, friends, community connections and a strong faith.

None of these things are mutually exclusive, you need a significant other in your life, your kids bring joy and your professional advancement brings confidence. It is all positive. The danger stems from putting too much emphasis in any one facet.

When people search for professional change, they really want life change. Do you wish you could inherit a million dollars right now?

What would you do with it?

What would you do with your time?

MOST people would answer "yes, yes," however, what they would continue to do or pursue in life, differs. A few would strive high and involve themselves in high risk activities, such as owning a restaurant or global travel. Would you deplete the money just as fast as you lost it?

Others would enjoy the "high life" and live everyday as if it were the last.

WHAT would you do?

Here is a life changing tip: Act like it is your last day and you can do whatever you want. What pursuit would make you most happy? What achievement could serve you best?

Nobody cares about your answer. YOU have to determine your path. If you had a bad child hood, you must now take responsibility; if you suffered disadvantages in life due to no fault of your own, you must take control and determine your future path.

Do it NOW. You do not need a counselor which becomes a rent a friend that you pay weekly. You do not need medications. You need to own your life. NOW: As it is.

The economy is ever-changing and it is a metaphor for life. Things can change in an instant and it does not matter if you are a male or female or you earn $50K or $500K, the difference is YOU.

Who am I to talk about this? I have experienced the in between; the highs and the lows and the human indifference. A life with and without addictions and a balanced life of achievement versus chaos are the goals. I do not know one person qualified to talk about life tha t has not both failed and succeeded. But, we are all a work in progress and that never changes, despite the realm we live in.

I urge you to take control of life as you know it now because it is ever-changing. We can make professional change and personal change ourselves. But, realize that sickness and health and good and evil are not our own creation and we cannot control the timeline.

How ridiculous would you feel if you spent all your years on professional advancement, only to find a personal illness controlling you into a short lived environment or if you compromised everything to care for someone who left you and that investment proved to leave you empty?

Fear of success is similar to <u>fear of failure</u>. They have many of the same symptoms, and both fears hold you back from achieving your dreams and goals.

Signs of Fear of Success

The biggest problem for many people is that their fear of success is largely unconscious. They just don't realize that they've been holding themselves back from doing something great.

If you experience the following thoughts or fears, you might have a fear of success on some level:

- You feel guilty about any success you have, no matter how small, because your friends, family, or co-workers haven't had the same success.
- You don't tell others about your accomplishments.
- You avoid or <u>procrastinate</u> on big projects, especially projects that could lead to recognition.
- You frequently <u>compromise</u> your own goals or agenda to avoid conflict in a group, or even conflict within your family.

- You <u>self-sabotage</u> your work or dreams by convincing yourself that you're not good enough to achieve either.
- You feel, subconsciously, that you don't deserve to enjoy success in your life.
- You believe that if you do achieve success, you won't be able to sustain it. Eventually you'll fail, and end up back in a worse place than from where you started. So you think, "why bother?"

Causes of Fear of Success

Fear of success has several possible causes:

- We fear what success will bring – for example, loneliness, new enemies, being isolated from our family, longer working hours, or being asked for favors or money.
- We're afraid that the higher we climb in life, the further we're going to fall when we make a mistake.
- We fear the added work, responsibilities, or criticism that we'll face.
- We fear that our relationships will suffer if we become successful. Our friends and family will react with jealousy and cynicism, and we'll lose the ones we love.

- We fear that accomplishing our goals, and realizing that we have the power to be successful, may actually cause an intense regret that we didn't act sooner.

Overcoming Fear of Success

You can use several different strategies to overcome your fear of success. The good news is that the more you face your fears, bring them to the surface, and analyze them rationally, the more you're likely to weaken those fears – and dramatically reduce your reluctance to achieve your goals.

Take a realistic look at what will happen if you succeed with your goal. Don't look at what you hope will happen, or what you fear will happen. Instead, look at what is likely to happen.

It's important not to give a quick answer to this. Take at least 15 minutes to examine the issues, and write down your answers to questions like these:

- How will my friends and family react if I accomplish this goal?
- How will my life change?

- What's the worst that could happen if I achieve this goal?
- What's the best that could happen?
- Why do I feel that I don't deserve to accomplish this goal?
- How motivated am I to work toward this goal?
- What am I currently doing to sabotage, or hurt, my own efforts?
- How can I stop those self-sabotaging behaviors?

Another useful technique is to address your fears directly, and then develop a backup plan that will overcome your concern.

## XXI. Staying Fired Up

After getting fired or losing your job in a lay off, it is easy to become emotionally depleted and succumb to a crisis of the spirit. This can be hedged of with a conscious effort to create or solidify a support group. A support group can consist of friends and family who can help to encourage you or provide networking opportunities. Support can also be derived from internet technology by exploring blogs which offer an opportunity to share experiences, anonymously, if preferred.

It is natural to feel a bit unsociable or an inclination to isolate until you can announce your newfound job, but this is not a cognitive, honest approach, it is reverting to going through the motions for appearances sake. WHO are you getting the job for? Is it to show others your worth or importance? Then, why not just ask whoever you are trying to impress, what job they would be dumbfounded if you attained?

The reason you do not use this methodology is because YOU are the one you must please and nobody else. Therefore, you must not avoid society nor should you place value on external judgements.

Since the daily routine of going to work is still fresh, try to recall the feelings of frustration when you were in a rut or experiencing difficulties in the workplace. Often, we tend to forget the troubled times only to enforce how much we miss having a job. This selective memory process is damaging and must be stopped in its tracks. Because your job search or career transition will most likely be a path of ups and downs. Some days may feel very productive, while other days may be filled with stress and anxiety.

Because life and job transition can be overwhelming, it is also vital to take control of those affected by this change. Talking to your children or other impacted family members is important, just as you would in a divorce, death or other jolting event.

Because children, especially, may feel the emotional stress in the household, it is vital that they understand that the parent did not do anything wrong and that job loss is an unfortunate, but normal event in life.

Also, let them know that while there may have to be some short-term changes, things are fine and will be on the upswing again.

If they are interested in helping and it is appropriate, you can educate them on the lessons of economic change by letting them take a temporary reduction in allowance or holding back on the purchase of something more expensive.

This will incorporate them into the experience directly and teach them valuable lessons to pull from in the future.

While you are dealing with the emotional and human factors in your time of transition, don't neglect the administrative necessities or they will add to your load and could increase your stress levels. The administrative items are anything from medical insurance to the creation or utilization of new email addresses or even general paperwork for unemployment or child support responsibilities.

Aside from involuntary job or life changes, many of us will facilitate the change on our own accord. In one of my transitions, I left my job, sold my house, moved 1,800 miles from Dallas to Boston only to move a couple of times in six months and interview with several companies from New York to New Hampshire and then decide I wanted to move to Europe and start my own business in a country with two languages I did not speak.

I was just out of my twenties and I didn't have children. In retrospect, it seems a little radical, but at the time, I felt I needed to shake things up a bit. I had been in Dallas, Texas for nearly a decade and things were not happening for me personally or professionally.

I know the saying "the grass is not always greener on the other side" often rings true, but I also believe it is necessary to recognize when you need to make a geographical or situational change. Intuition probably speaks to you long before you decide to make a move.

I felt empowered moving to the Northeast, but made another immediate change based on my professional track. I decided to buy an American franchise in Spain. I was drawn to the business as it was woman focused and the fitness aspect interested appealed to me as I had been fit in the past and wanted that again, along with the European experience.

However, pushing so far out of my comfort zone and going to a foreign country to make an investment with my life savings was a challenge.

I did have a supportive partner and some resources available to me at the time, but often people do not talk about their struggles openly, so it is easy to feel isolated.

If you don't have access to multiple support systems, such as family, friends, therapists, recruiters, life coaches, spiritual leaders, etc., you have to create an inner system of support and try to visualize your life as if it is a movie. You are the producer and you have the power to edit as you act in your life everyday.

Sometimes life change comes in the form of starting a family. While men and women have different roles in that starting of a family, it is life altering and as many suggest that while you can be prepared to a certain extent, you won't fully know understand the significant changes it brings until you experience it firsthand.

Again, I suggest ready valuable guide books and utilizing any tool you have to prepare for this experience.

Even the best changes or transitions in life cost you in the form of blood, sweat and tears. When starting your own business, it is this "sweat equity" that is so rewarding.

Everyone has a bucket list, a list of all the things you would like to do and experience in life. Nobody in his or her right mind would list the desire to lose a job, but for those who have gone through this, they can tell you that it often turns out to be the best thing to ever happen to them.

Like many, I had "Run a Marathon before 30" on my bucket list. I ran track and cross country in high school and I enjoyed running and it seemed like the ultimate challenge. Thirty came and went and ironically, it was not until I had a two year old daughter that I ran and completed my first marathon.

It is very true about life being in the journey as I shed a lot of sweat and tears before I finished.

There is no good time to lose a job, but you make the best of it and keep moving ahead, just like with running. I ended up running a marathon before 40 and when I had just started a family, so timing seemingly not ideal, but it was on my own terms.

Most of it was on my own terms. I flew to Palma de Mallorca with my family in the hopes of making a short family holiday around the day of the marathon. After a long day of travel and adventure, I retired and made sure my iPod was in the off mode. What I didn't know was that my then two year old had played with it the entire time on the plane and when I turned it on the next morning just minutes to my start time, I had zero battery left.

I knew I had about five hours of running ahead and I felt like giving up, but I had trained hard and knew I had to keep moving. It was difficult and the sunny day turned to rain for the last two straight hours. I crossed the finish line with ear plugs in, sunglasses on, grabbed my medal and walked to a cafe to meet up with my husband, daughter and friends. I was depleted, but invigorated at the same time and I realized that you must endure the blood, sweat and tears in order to embrace the small joys and pinnacle moments in life.

I want to share these experiences and the visual tools and guides with the hopes that anyone reading this can continue moving forward through challenging life transitions and changes.

Keep the momentums moving forward and you can be assured it will pay-off. The end result may be different than what you envisioned, but things will get better.

Understand that these challenging events will only be a snapshot in the montage of your life. If you think of it in these terms you take away the power that any one event has one your life.

If you continue to work the process, enjoy the journey and continue an honest internal dialogue, you will stay **FIRED UP!**

AUTHOR UPDATE:

Since the first edition of this book was written in 2007, the global economy has been in a whirlwind of chaos. I have lived in Spain over a decade, the Eurozone's fourth largest economy, and I have experienced the second recession in three years. Prime Minister Mariano Rajoy currently seeks more austerity measures and is considering the request of a Euro-zone led bailout.

While I continue to work a contract I have with the United States remotely, I know that it will not last forever. The degree of FLEXIBILITY and stamina needed for our modern world is high. I have altered my work space to reflect our global market and I have relied less on my current geography. I continue to savor the Mediterranean diet and stay FIRED UP!

## XXII. Credits:

(explanations: Please report citation or reference errors to ashleigh@ashleighrussell.com).

1. Martinez-Granado, Maite, 2002. "**Self-Employment and Labour Market Transitions: A Multiple State Model**," CEPR Discussion Papers 3661, C.E.P.R. Discussion Papers.
2. Hannu Tervo, 2006. "**Regional unemployment, self-employment and family background**," Applied Economics, Taylor and Francis Journals, vol. 38(9), pages 1055-1062, May.
3. Federico S. Mandelman & Gabriel V. Montes Rojas, 2007. "**Microentrepreneurship and the business cycle: is self-employment a desired outcome?**," Working Paper 2007-15, Federal Reserve Bank of Atlanta.
4. Lin, Zhengxi & Picot, Garnett & Yates, Janice, 1999. "**The Entry and Exit Dynamics of Self-employment in Canada**," Analytical Studies Branch Research Paper Series 1999134e, Statistics Canada, Analytical Studies Branch.
5. Daniela Glocker & Viktor Steiner, 2007. "**Self-Employment - a Way to End Unemployment? : Empirical Evidence from German Pseudo-Panel Data**," Discussion Papers of DIW Berlin 661, DIW Berlin, German Institute for Economic Research. Other versions: Daniela Glocker & Viktor Steiner, 2007. "**Self-Employment: A Way to End Unemployment? Empirical Evidence from German Pseudo-Panel Data**," IZA Discussion Papers 2561, Institute for the Study of Labor (IZA).
6. Olympia Bover & Ramón Gómez, 2004. "**Another look at unemployment duration: exit to a permanent vs. a temporary job**," Investigaciones Economicas, Fundación SEPI, vol. 28(2), pages 285-314, May.
7. Blázquez, Maite, 2005. "**"Low-wage Employment and Mobility in Spain"**," Working Papers in Economic Theory 2005/03, Universidad Autónoma de Madrid (Spain), Department of Economic Analysis (Economic Theory and Economic History).

8. Raquel Carrasco & Mette Ejrnæs, 2003. "**Self-employment in Denmark and Spain: Institution, Economic Conditions and Gender differences**," CAM Working Papers 2003-06, University of Copenhagen. Department of Economics. Centre for Applied Microeconometrics.
9. Niittykangas, Hannu & Tervo, Hannu, 2002. "**Intergenerational mobility in self-employment: a regional approach**," ERSA conference papers ersa02p350, European Regional Science Association.
10. Amelie Constant & Klaus F. Zimmermann, 2004. "**Self-Employment Dynamics across the Business Cycle : Migrants versus Natives**," Discussion Papers of DIW Berlin 455, DIW Berlin, German Institute for Economic Research. Other versions:
11. Hannu Tervo, 2004. "**Self-employment dynamics in rural and urban labour markets**," ERSA conference papers ersa04p396, European Regional Science Association. Ellen Rissman, 2003. "**Self-employment as an alternative to unemployment**," Working Paper Series WP-03-34, Federal Reserve Bank of Chicago.
12. Marco Caliendo & Alexander S. Kritikos, 2008. "**Start-Ups by the Unemployed: Characteristics, Survival and Direct Employment Effects**," Working Papers 008, Hanseatic University, Germany, Department of Economics.
Other versions: Marco Caliendo & Alexander S. Kritikos, 2007. "**Start-Ups by the Unemployed: Characteristics, Survival and Direct Employment Effects**," IZA Discussion Papers 3220, Institute for the Study of Labor (IZA). Douglas Holtz-Eakin & Harvey Rosen, 1999. "**Cash Constraints and Business Start-ups: Deutschmarks versus Dollars**," Center for Policy Research Working Papers 11, Center for Policy Research, Maxwell School, Syracuse University.
13. Hannu Tervo & Mika Haapanen, 2005. "**Self-employment duration in urban and rural locations**," ERSA conference papers ersa05p315, European Regional Science Association. Reize, Frank, 2000. "**Leaving unemployment for self-employment : a discrete duration analysis of determinants and stability of self-employment among former unemployed**," ZEW Discussion

Papers 00-26, ZEW - Zentrum für Europäische Wirtschaftsforschung / Center for European Economic Research.
14. Fernando Munoz-Bullon & Begona Cueto Iglesias, 2008. "**The sustainability of start-up firms among formerly wage workers**," Business Economics Working Papers wb083108, Universidad Carlos III, Departamento de Econom
15. Vecchione, Patrice, 2001. "**Writing and the Spiritual Life**,"

XXIII. Notes:

Notes:

Notes:

Notes:

Notes:

Notes:

Notes:

Notes:

Notes:

Notes:

Notes:

Notes:

Notes:

Notes:

Notes:

Notes:

Notes:

Notes:

Notes:

Made in the USA
Lexington, KY
01 September 2019